Original title:
The Lunar Limericks

Copyright © 2025 Creative Arts Management OÜ
All rights reserved.

Author: Juliette Kensington
ISBN HARDBACK: 978-1-80567-776-5
ISBN PAPERBACK: 978-1-80567-897-7

Witty Wanderings

A rabbit hopped with flair,
His top hat flew in the air.
He danced under the moon,
To a comical tune.

A grouchy old cat said, "Beware!"
But snickers filled up the square.
With each silly twirl,
The whole crowd would whirl.

Moonlit Mirth

An owl who loved to sing high,
Tried juggling fish pie in the sky.
With each toss and flip,
He took quite a dip—

The fish splashed down with a sigh.
The stars winked down from above,
As laughter spread all around,
A true moonlit sound.

Cheerful Cosmos

A cow in a rocket took flight,
With dreams of a starry night.
She mooed at the suns,
And danced with her buns—

While planets spun left and right.
All comets rolled back with glee,
As she shared her cheese fondue,
Now that's cosmic stew!

Ephemeral Elegance

A snail with a bow tie so grand,
Took a stroll through the soft, moonlit sand.
His pace was quite slow,
Yet style's all aglow,

As he wiggled with grace at the band.
A butterfly laughed, saying, "Wow!"
"That snail is a dandy!" they vow,
With a twirl and a bow.

Jesters of the Night Sky

In the dark where the stars play,
A moonbeam juggles night away.
With laughs and chuckles loud,
    It dances for the crowd.

A comet zips, a shooting star,
Tells jokes from places near and far.
The planets chuckle, too,
    In this cosmic comedy crew.

Glistening Grins of Night

The night unveils a silver show,
With laughter riding on the glow.
Stars twinkle in delight,
As they share tales of flight.

A squirrel on a moonlit spree,
Searching for a cosmic tree.
With a wink and a nod,
It teases the night, quite odd!

Lunar Larks

Up above where the giggles soar,
Lunar larks sing forevermore.
Chasing shadows in the sky,
On their bicycles, they fly.

They tumble through a fluffy cloud,
Riding laughs, they sing out loud.
With every twist and turn,
The humor's theirs to earn!

Jestful Reflections

Reflections gleam on the moonlit lake,
A gaggle of frogs, a hearty quake.
They croak their jokes with glee,
In a wacky harmony.

The owls hoot with jest and cheer,
As the night draws everyone near.
Laughter echoes through the trees,
Carried softly on the breeze.

Celestial Antics

A cow jumped high in the night,
It thought it could reach the moon's light.
But with a loud thud,
It fell in the mud,
Now it just watches the bright.

Jovial Moondance

A rabbit donned dance shoes so red,
Twisting and leaping, it sped.
The stars sang along,
With giggles so strong,
While critters all jived in a thread.

Celestial Capers

Two squirrels stole cheese from a kite,
They soared in a whimsical flight.
But up in the sky,
They heard a loud cry,
And fell with a plop—what a sight!

Gleeful Full Moon

The moon wore a hat made of cheese,
It teased all the stars with a breeze.
They wiggled and swayed,
In a rhythm, they played,
As owls hooted tunes through the trees.

Cosmic Rhymes

In space there lived a green frog,
He danced on a bright shiny log.
He twirled with the stars,
Shouting, 'Look at my cars!'

His friends wore hats made of cheese,
While they floated along with such ease.
They giggled and joked,
As the universe poked.

Each comet brought laughter and glee,
As they sipped on zero-gravity tea.
Why fly with such fuss,
When they could ride the bus?

So if you hear chuckles at night,
It's the frogs causing all of the fright.
In the skies, they prance,
In their cosmic dance.

Giggling at Twilight

A squirrel tried to glide from the moon,
But fell with a loud, funny swoon.
He landed with flair,
In a big fluffy chair,

And shouted, "I'll sketch a cartoon!"
With a quill made of starlight and cheese,
He drew silly suns,
And raced with the puns,

While giggling at twilight's cool breeze.
His friends joined the fun in a line,
They fashioned a plot so divine,
They played hide and seek,
With a bright shooting streak,

And laughed till the sun chose to shine!

Starlit Satire

Under a sky full of sparkly dreams,
A penguin wore glasses, or so it seems.
He read from a book,
With a rather strange look,

On irony woven in beams.
The stars winked in mischievous ways,
They twirled through the dark, full of praise.
With a wink and a nod,
They danced on the sod,

Floating softly like wisps in a haze.
So if you hear giggles at night,
It's the celestial jesters, in flight.
They prank and they tease,
In the cosmic breeze.

Laughing with the Moonbeams

A cat in a rocket ship zoomed,
As the whole galaxy lightly entombed.
With a laugh and a purr,
He caused quite a stir,

While the stars in their orbits consumed.
He caught a few beams as they sailed,
For a ride that was surely prevailed.
With giggles and cheer,
Every planet would hear,

His tales of mischief unveiled.
So if you hear laughter all around,
Know the joy of the cosmos is found.
With a pounce and a cheer,
They spread good vibes near,
And kept the night sky unbound.

Moonlit Whispers

Under the glow of the moon's delight,
Cats hold a dance, quite a sight.
They prance and they leap,
In shadows they creep,
Making the nighttime feel bright.

A raccoon with a mask takes a chance,
In the moonlight, he joins in the dance.
With a cheeky little grin,
He dips and he spins,
Inviting all critters to prance.

Celestial Jests

A cow jumped over the crescent's edge,
Making a deal with a starry hedge.
"I'll leap if you cheer,
And bring some more beer,
For laughs, we'll push limits to pledge!"

An owl wore a hat that was blue,
Claiming he'd found it from a zoo.
He hooted with glee,
"It's fashionable, see?"
And thus started the night's silly review.

Night's Silvery Verse

Bats in sunglasses, oh what a sight,
Gliding around, having late-night flight.
They throw a surprise,
With witty wisecries,
Filling the air with pure lighthearted bite.

A frog broke into song with flair,
As fireflies twinkled in midair.
He croaked just for fun,
Under stars, everyone,
Joined in the chorus without a care.

Hilarity Under the Moon

A weasel in stripes claimed to skate,
Gliding on puddles, wasn't that great?
He slipped and fell hard,
But laughed, not disbarred,
"Next time, I'll bring something more straight!"

A possum held court, quite the scene,
Telling tales that were silly and mean.
With a wink and a jest,
Made the midnight the best,
In the fun that the night could convene.

Jovial Skylines

In the night sky, stars like to prance,
They gossip and twirl in a cosmic dance.
The moon winks with glee,
While comets agree,
It's time for a radiant, raucous romance.

Yo-yoing planets, all merry and bright,
They twist and they swirl, what a comical sight!
With laughter so loud,
They rally a crowd,
Turning starlit dreams into sheer delight.

Cackles with the Cosmos

A star bumped a comet, said, "Watch out, friend!"
With a whoosh and a whistle, they started to bend.
Through giggles and beams,
They plotted wild schemes,
Creating a jest that would never end.

The space dust erupted with chuckles and cheer,
As galaxies spun while they all gathered near.
Shooting stars took a bow,
As black holes said, "Wow!"
In a raucous, hilarious cosmic frontier.

Nectar of Nighttime

In twilight's embrace, fireflies light the show,
They tickle the air with a luminous glow.
With nectar so sweet,
They prance on their feet,
Creating a buzz as they flit to and fro.

The owls in their wisdom hoot softly with mirth,
Their jokes drift around, bringing joy on the earth.
The sun bids adieu,
As twilight shines through,
With laughter and light, they know what they're worth.

Chuckles in the Celestial Realm

In the depths of the void, a giggling whole,
Where quarks do a jig and dark matter rolls.
The photons toast up,
As starlight erupts,
In a universe bursting with jovial souls.

Each planet tells tales that twist and defy,
With funny old legends that never run dry.
From Saturn's bold rings,
To Mars and its flings,
The cosmos just chuckles, oh my, oh my!

Night's Playful Muse

In the sky where shadows dance,
A cat in moonlight takes a chance.
She leaps with glee,
Mice shout, "Not me!"
This night's a whimsical romance.

The owls hoot tunes from the trees,
While fireflies buzz with such ease.
They flicker and glow,
As if in a show,
A sparkle that aims to please.

A raccoon dons a top hat bright,
Stealing snacks under the moon's light.
He tips with charm,
Brings quite the alarm,
Who knew that he could delight?

So raise a toast to night's delight,
Where laughter takes off in flight.
With giggles and grins,
Let joy be our sins,
In this charming, silly twilight.

Grins of the Gibbous

Oh, the moon is quite a sight,
Casting shadows deep and bright.
A squirrel pretends,
With acorns as friends,
They're chattering through the night.

The stars twinkle back with glee,
Joining in the lunacy spree.
With a wink and a nod,
It feels rather odd,
When comets start dancing free.

A frog with a crown takes a leap,
Reciting the secrets he keeps.
"Ribbit and cheer,
I'll draw you near,
Stay with me while the world sleeps!"

So savor this silly jest,
With laughter, we're truly blessed.
The gibbous moon beams,
Fueling our dreams,
As night unfolds her best!

Starlit Jingles

Beneath the moon's bright, cheery face,
A mouse found a crystal place.
He swirled and he twirled,
In his shiny world,
With laughter jumping in space.

The stars sang a catchy tune,
As crickets played soft in June.
They snapped their small feet,
In a dance that's sweet,
Under the watchful moon's boon.

A pig in pajamas ran wild,
Chasing fireflies, oh, how he smiled!
He slipped on some dew,
With a splash, "Who knew?"
That being silly feels so mild.

So join in the sounds of the night,
Let laughter take off in flight.
With every neat twirl,
And giggle, we whirl,
Gathered in starlit delight.

Silvery Nonsense

Under the silver glow we roam,
Turtles in top hats call it home.
They waddle and sway,
In a zany way,
Making the moon feel like Rome.

Kangaroos jump with a silly flair,
While raccoons play tag in the air.
With giggles and squeaks,
All night it peaks,
In a world that's beyond compare.

The stars wink down, "Join our fun!"
A parade has only begun.
With laughter up high,
We'll dance in the sky,
As night turns to morning sun.

So let's share this whimsical night,
Wearing joy as our brilliant light.
With stories to tell,
And laughter that swells,
In silvery nonsense, we delight.

Moonlit Malarkey

A rabbit once danced on the moon,
In a suit made of fluff, quite a tune.
He tripped on a star,
And giggled from far,
As the craters sang back, 'What a spoon!'

A cat with a hat rode a beam,
Claiming he was the moon's finest dream.
He slid with great flair,
Through the soft silver air,
And said, 'Who could resist such a scheme?'

A cow tried to jump over high,
But ended up stuck in the sky.
With comets in tow,
She mooed soft and low,
Saying, 'I'll surely give this a try!'

In shadows, the owls had a ball,
Telling jokes to the stars, one and all.
With giggles and hoots,
They danced in their boots,
Underneath the moon's silvery pall.

Spontaneous Stardust

A star sneezed and sprinkled some dust,
Creating a galaxy's rust.
With laughter so bright,
They giggled all night,
Proclaiming, 'This glitter we trust!'

A comet with flair made a splash,
Zipping past with a colorful crash.
The planets all laughed,
'Twas the best kind of craft,
As stardust flew by in a flash!

An alien chef made a pie,
With ingredients found way up high.
Each slice brought a cheer,
As it flew 'round with beer,
'Twas a feast 'neath the bright, twinkling sky!

On Saturn, there's dancing all day,
While moons twirl with comets in play.
With rings made of song,
The laughter was strong,
As they spun in their waltz far away.

Moon's Mirthful Musings

A wise old moon pondered at night,
How a chicken could take such a flight.
With space suits and dreams,
Through the star-spangled beams,
She chuckled, 'What's wrong with this sight?'

A squirrel rode rockets with glee,
While singing a tune with a tree.
As he zipped 'round the stars,
He sent jokes to Mars,
And danced with the stardust so free!

Two stars had a game of charades,
They fought with their cosmic cascades.
Though comets sped by,
Their laughter would fly,
In a nebula filled with parades!

The moon's face contorted with grin,
Watching all of these fun things begin.
With a twinkle so clear,
She raised up a cheer,
'Oh, the joy that we find in our spin!'

School of Moonbeams

In a school where the moonbeams play,
The students would giggle all day.
With lessons in flight,
And how stars shine bright,
Their laughter would echo away!

The teacher, a wise old space cat,
Taught the kids to balance on that.
With a hop and a skip,
And a twirl in the trip,
'Now here's how to land, not just chat!'

A goat in a space suit wore shoes,
Said 'Dancing on comets, I choose!'
With each glittery bound,
He spread joy all around,
While munching on stardusty news!

In moonlit classrooms, they dreamt,
With ideas so grandly they schemed.
Through laughter and fun,
Their hearts all were one,
In the universe's fanciful stream!

Rhymes Under the Moon

A cow jumped high in the night,
She slipped and gave quite a fright,
With a leap and a bound,
She rolled on the ground,
And everyone laughed at the sight.

A cat wore a hat made of cheese,
It smelled, and it made people sneeze,
With a wiggle and twist,
Not a chance was missed,
As laughter danced on with the breeze.

An owl hooted loud in delight,
As he took a stroll in the light,
With his friends all around,
Joyful sounds were found,
Winging joy 'til the end of the night.

And thus, in the glow's gentle tune,
We'll dance 'neath the bright silver moon,
With giggles in tow,
And a humorous flow,
We'll laugh with the stars as our boon.

Moonbeam Merriment

A frog in a suit took a leap,
He landed in puddles so deep,
With a splash and a cheer,
To all those who hear,
His antics make nighttime less sleep.

A raccoon tried dancing a jig,
But slipped on a big, soggy twig,
With a tumble so bright,
He rolled 'til twilight,
And the critters all laughed at his gig.

Two fireflies flashed with such glee,
Playing tag in the glow of the spree,
With a flick and a wink,
They zoomed without think,
Chasing dreams 'neath the grand tamarind tree.

So come join the fun through the night,
As we chuckle 'neath stars shining bright,
With a wink and a grin,
Let the laughter begin,
Just a joyous, whimsical sight.

Celestial Chuckles

A squirrel in pajamas took flight,
Dove into a nut-filled delight,
With a crunch and a chew,
He danced as he blew,
His friends into giggles outright.

A penguin slid down a steep hill,
On a skateboard he made with great skill,
With a clang and a crash,
He made quite a splash,
As laughter rang out with a thrill.

A bunny wore shoes made of cake,
He hopped with a smile, not a quake,
With each bounce and twist,
Through the moonlit mist,
He brought joy no one could forsake.

Let's raise up our cups to the cheer,
To the mischief that brings us all near,
With stories retold,
As we laugh and behold,
Life's moments we cherish right here.

Laughter Beneath the Stars

A chicken who fancied a race,
Danced 'round with so much grace,
But tripped on a mat,
Where she squeaked like a cat,
And giggles erupted in space.

A hedgehog dressed up for a show,
With glitter and sparkles to glow,
But slipped on a shoe,
With a wild ballyhoo,
And laughter erupted in flow.

Two bears tried to tango at night,
Their moves brought the stars pure delight,
With a twirl and a spin,
They fell with a grin,
A soft landing, all fuzzy and bright.

So gather 'neath skies filled with glee,
With friends underneath the grand tree,
Let's share in the fun,
And laugh everyone,
For joy is the key, can't you see?

Twilight's Rhyming Riddles

In twilight's soft embrace, it seems,
The moon plays tricks on sleepy dreams.
She winks with golden light,
Inviting stars to take flight.

The owls hoot tales from the trees,
While fireflies buzz with giddy ease.
A cat on a fence gives a shout,
'What's this silly fuss all about?'

A rabbit hops with flair and grace,
Wearing a hat, oh what a face!
He juggles carrots in the air,
While a crowd of mice stop and stare.

With giggles echoing through the night,
Join the moon in her merry flight.
Laughing shadows dance and twirl,
As dreams are spun in a sparkling whirl.

Gloaming Giggles

As gloaming paints the sky with cheer,
The moon drops in, oh dear, oh dear!
It tickles clouds with a beam,
Spreading laughter like a dream.

A frog croaks jokes by the stream,
While crickets form a singing team.
They croon to stars, all twinkling bright,
Creating melodies of pure delight.

A mouse in shoes spins round and round,
While giggles bounce from the ground.
He shimmies through the soft, cool grass,
Making every moment a joyous pass.

In this evening's playful glow,
The world spins fast, but soft and slow.
So let your worries drift away,
And join the night's enchanting play.

The Playful Orb

Oh playful orb in midnight sky,
With silver beams, you seem to fly.
You tease the night, dance with glee,
While shadows join your jubilee.

A squirrel dons a tiny hat,
And dances 'neath the moonlight's pat.
He twirls with grace, a twist, a spin,
With laughter bubbling from within.

A porcupine plays peek-a-boo,
His quills all shiny, sparkling new.
He laughs and rolls, a joyous sight,
Making merry in the moon's soft light.

With every bounce and every leap,
The night grows full of giggling peep.
So join the fun, don't hesitate,
For in this moment, love's the fate.

A Dance of Delight

A dance begins when night takes hold,
With moonbeams shimmering like gold.
The stars align, a lively crowd,
As giggles rise, both soft and loud.

A bear in shades sways side to side,
With a twangy tune that won't subside.
The rabbits join with a hop and skip,
And weave their magic with every tip.

A parade of critters fills the night,
With twirling tails, it's pure delight.
The fireflies blink, a rhythm fine,
Lighting the stage for moonlit shine.

So join the dance, don't be shy,
Under the stars, let laughter fly.
For in this moment, hearts unite,
In a dance of joy, oh, what a sight!

Laughter in the Dark

In the night when the moon likes to shine,
A raccoon danced on a line so fine.
He tripped with a clatter,
His friends all a-chatter,
As he tumbled into the pine.

The owls hooted loud, quite a song,
In the woods where the shadows belong.
A frog joined the fun,
With a leap and a run,
They chirped until daylight was strong.

Then a bat swooped by, looking sleek,
With a wink and a giggle so cheek.
He spun round and round,
Made a sweet, silly sound,
And all of the creatures would peek.

As the sun started painting the skies,
They bid farewell, with laughter and sighs.
In the glow of the morn,
Not a frown could be worn,
Just smiles and some twinkly goodbyes.

Moonbeam Musings

In the glow of a bright silver light,
A cat tried to dance, what a sight!
With a wiggle and pounce,
She'd twirl and they'd bounce,
Her moves brought the stars pure delight.

Then a turtle in shades came to play,
He grooved on his back in a sway.
With a shell full of cheer,
He'd glide, never fear,
As night turned to dawn's soft array.

A bright comet zipped through the scene,
Waving hello, bright and keen.
It sparked laughter loud,
To a critter crowd,
With joy that was truly serene.

As the moon took a bow, nice and slow,
The critters all clapped in a row.
With giggles abound,
In this funny round,
They'd carry the laughter aglow.

Whimsy Among the Stars

There once was a star with a hat,
Who fancied himself quite a brat.
He twinkled with glee,
And shouted, 'Come see!'
As he juggled the moon like a cat.

A snail said, 'Now how can that be?'
While munching on lettuce with glee.
He chuckled and sighed,
Then gracefully glided,
'Catch your dreams, just let them fly free!'

A rabbit hopped high with delight,
He whispered to stars in the night.
'The fun never ends,
With my cosmic friends,
We wiggle and wiggle in flight!'

As the dawn started mixing the hues,
The stars shared their best, quirky news.
With laughter and cheer,
They'd gathered quite near,
Spreading giggles like morning dew.

Playful Reflections

There's a pond where the moon likes to bathe,
With frogs who all sing, bold and brave.
They leap with a splash,
In a whimsical dash,
Creating reflections that wave.

A fish with a grin flips around,
While the lilies all wiggle, profound.
With bubbles that pop,
And giggles that hop,
They swim in the laughter they found.

The crickets join in with a tune,
As they dance with the light of the moon.
With a hop and a skip,
They all take a dip,
In a chorus that makes spirits swoon.

When the twilight begins to descend,
With each whisper, the fun will not end.
In the moon's gentle glow,
Laughter will flow,
As new tales and giggles they send.

Cosmic Capers

A cat on a comet took flight,
With snacks made of cheese to ignite.
It danced through the stars,
With chortles and bars,
Chasing asteroids all through the night.

An alien friend joined the spree,
Dressed in a sparkly sea.
They both found a crew,
Of frogs colored blue,
Juggling comets while sipping on tea.

They twirled with a giggle and cheer,
Telling tales that only they'd hear.
With a wink and a nod,
They flew like a god,
Leaving meteor trails that were clear.

Then suddenly, with quite a loud pop,
The cat took a tumble, a drop.
But up in the air,
Without a care,
It laughed and just shouted, "Don't stop!"

Rhymes among the Night

In a rocket-shaped shoe lived a goat,
That dreamt it could swim, not just float.
It splashed with delight,
In a pool made of light,
While wearing a fabulous coat.

A squirrel with a top hat arrived,
With rhymes that had everyone jived.
They danced on the moon,
To a soft, silly tune,
As stardust and laughter connived.

A bear brought some honey, quite sweet,
To share with the crowd at their feet.
They dipped to the beat,
As the night turned complete,
With giggles and snacks, oh so neat!

As dawn peeked through clouds, what a sight!
The friends bid farewell with delight.
With a wink and a wave,
They knew they'd be brave,
To meet up again in the night.

Celestial Glee

A tiny green bug in a ship,
Took off for a galactic trip.
With wings made of cheese,
It flew in the breeze,
And danced with a comet's bright flip.

It met with a frog, quite absurd,
Who sang with a laugh, not a word.
They hopped through the air,
Without any care,
In a galaxy swirling and blurred.

The stars cheered them on in their play,
While the planets all joined in the fray.
With joy, they declared,
"This fun must be shared!"
As they twirled and twinkled away.

But soon, the moon yawned, oh so wide,
And the bug knew it couldn't abide.
With a wave and a grin,
They promised to spin,
Underneath the night tide as they hide.

Whimsy in the Wane

An owl donned a pair of bright specs,
While reading some odd silly texts.
It hooted with glee,
As it hosted a tea,
For critters adorned with tinsel checks.

A hedgehog brought cupcakes galore,
That spun as they rolled on the floor.
With frosting that glowed,
The guests overflowed,
And laughter sang out evermore.

A party of stars joined the play,
In costumes so wild, bright, and gay.
They twirled in the sky,
With a wink and a sigh,
As shadows gave way to the day.

With hearts full of joy, they all cheered,
For the friendships that nobody feared.
In the echo of night,
They found pure delight,
And memories that never disappeared.

Nighttime Nuances

A cat on the roof, in the moonlight,
Wears glasses and thinks he's quite bright.
He prowls with such flair,
Floating light as a chair.

The stars giggle softly above,
At squirrels who dance with a shove.
They trip and they fall,
Yet still have a ball,

And owls hoot in rhythm tonight,
While fireflies flash bits of delight.
With candles aglow,
They set quite the show.

As bedtime draws near, don't you fear,
For mischief awaits with a cheer.
So laugh if you might,
In this whimsical night.

Radiant Rhymes

A rabbit with dreams of high flight,
Wore a cape made of silver so bright.
He hopped on the lawn,
Till the break of dawn,

With jokes that made everyone laugh,
He pranced like a silly giraffe.
With each little joke,
Laughter softly woke,

There's a mouse who can dance on a dime,
He twirls and he flips, oh, so fine.
In shadows, he swings,
Adding joy that he brings.

As crickets trill in perfect time,
Filling night with a soft, sweet rhyme.
In moon's gentle glow,
Giggles flow like a show.

Stellar Shenanigans

A raccoon, clad in glittery bling,
Tries to dance but can't find a fling.
He spins and he twirls,
In a dress made of pearls,

While meteors race in the night,
Each one putting on quite a sight.
They streak with such flair,
Like they haven't a care.

There are turtles who play in a band,
Creating a sound that's so grand.
With drums made of leaves,
And songs that deceives,

As laughter and music combine,
In a world where the stars brightly shine.
So giggle and sway,
In this nighttime ballet.

Mirthful Moonscapes

A hedgehog wore shoes made of cheese,
He wobbled and tripped with such ease.
He danced 'neath the glow,
Of the moon, oh-so low,

While frogs in a chorus did sing,
With splashes and jumps, they take wing.
Each croak fills the air,
A delightful affair.

Two penguins, just out for a roam,
Found a patch of blue sea as their home.
They waddle and glide,
Who knew they could ride?

And stars wink at troublemakers bold,
As shenanigans quietly unfold.
In this night's parade,
Joyously displayed.

Midnight Riddles

At midnight's stroke, the owls all cheer,
They trade their tales for a pint of beer.
A mouse in a hat,
Gives secrets to a cat,
Who swears she won't tell, but we know she's queer.

The stars above twinkle with glee,
As crickets play jump rope by a tree.
A frog starts to trip,
With a clumsy flip,
While fireflies buzz their minds free.

With shadows that dance on the ground,
And whispers of laughter abound.
A toad croaks a joke,
Amidst all the smoke,
As laughter in moonlight is found.

So gather your friends for a night,
Where giggles eclipse the moonlight.
We'll puzzle and jest,
And forget all the rest,
Till dawn brings a tickle, not fright.

Enchanted Lunar Laughter

Beneath the moon's grin, we gather near,
With jokes to make everyone cheer.
A squirrel in pants,
Joins in with his dance,
As laughter echoes sweet and clear.

A hedgehog plays drums on a log,
While fireflies glow like a smog.
The rabbits all sing,
Of the joy that they bring,
To a night that feels like a dialogue.

With each silly tale, we can see,
The whimsy that flows like a spree.
The stars nod and wink,
At the funny clink,
Of giggles and glances carefree.

A raccoon with flair made a hat,
Declared himself king of the spat.
With each roaring burst,
The moon too, immersed,
Held court for the creatures, just that.

The Moon's Mischief

The moon played a trick on the tide,
It swirled and it dipped with pride.
A fish in a bow,
Said, "Hey, watch me go!"
As waves laughed and bubbled beside.

A possum on stilts tried to skate,
A crowd gathered, thinking it great.
But he slipped on a shell,
With a comical yell,
Now he's famous—his fall was first-rate!

Balloons floated high in the night,
As pumpkins joined in the delight.
A bat wore a tie,
And gave it a try,
For a high-flying jig, what a sight!

The night wore a cloak made of fun,
Each creature out there on the run.
When laughter's a game,
You'll never feel shame,
'Cause mischief can't help but outrun!

Sylvan Serenades

In the forest where shadows play tricks,
A bear learns to juggle with sticks.
With a wink and a grin,
He starts to spin,
While birds join the fun with their flicks.

A turtle with shades had a dream,
To dance to a whimsical theme.
He grooved on his shell,
With a jiggly yell,
And startled a fish from the stream.

The sprites all chimed in with their glee,
As laughter rang out from each tree.
With giggles and cheers,
They conquered their fears,
As joy floated high on the spree.

So gather, dear friends, by the brook,
For tales that will leave you all shook.
In the moon's charming light,
We'll revel tonight,
For humor's the sweetest of hooks.

Jokes at Midnight

In the dark, the moonlight beams,
Crickets laugh in silly dreams.
A cat wearing a top hat,
Says, "I'm the king of the mat!"

Stars giggle, they can't keep still,
A hedgehog slips on a hill.
With a wink, the raccoon scolds,
"Where's your sense of fun, goldfish?"

The owls hoot a punchline new,
The fireflies twinkle, "What's due?"
A skunk cracks a joke so bold,
It's one that never gets old!

Why did the bat join the band?
To strum with a bushy-tailed hand!
At midnight, laughter surrounds,
In this land where joy abounds!

Eclipsed Echoes

When the moon hides away in fright,
The stars whisper jokes through the night.
"Why did the comet flee?"
"To catch up with glee, you see!"

Planets chuckle, spinning around,
While a cow jumps over the ground.
"What's an astronaut's snack?"
"A lunar cheese hack!"

Shadows dance in ebullient glee,
As the sun has a coffee, you see.
The echoes of giggles abound,
In this cosmic playground found!

But once the sun starts to peek,
All the funny stars start to sneak.
"See you next time, dear moon friend!"
"Until the eclipse, we'll pretend!"

Jovial Nocturne

Underneath the silvery glow,
A squirrel tells tales of woe.
"Why did the owl cry at night?
Too much cheese gave it a fright!"

The breeze carries whispers of fun,
As foxes gather, itching to run.
"What's a vampire's favorite song?
Something to hum with a throng!"

The pond reflects a giggling frog,
Who jokes that he's a nighttime hog.
"Why take a bath on the moon?
To make sure you smell like a tune!"

With laughter bouncing through the trees,
The moon sways gently in the breeze.
"Let's plan a party come next dark!
With funny tales that will leave a mark!"

The Moon's Witty Revels

Atop the hills, the moon beams bright,
With tales that tickle just right.
"What did the star say to the moon?
You're my favorite dancing tune!"

A rabbit joins in with a joke,
"A shadow must laugh, or it'll choke!"
The trees sway to the rhythm of cheer,
As the night air fills with laughter clear.

A dog wearing shades takes a stand,
"Why do I get a sunny band?
Because I bark in the party light,
And groove away into the night!"

Echoes dance across silver seas,
While the night shares secrets with ease.
With each chuckle and every cheer,
The moon's witty revels draw near!

Lighthearted Luminosity

In the night sky, a cheese wheel flies,
Mice in space, oh what a surprise!
They dance on the beams,
Creating wild dreams,
With laughter that echoes and sighs.

Stars wink at the silly moon,
A jazzy, bright, glowing tune.
They sway to the beat,
With light-hearted feet,
As they party all night till June.

A rabbit hops high in the glow,
Wearing shades and a stylish bow.
He jumps with great flair,
With friends everywhere,
In a garden where cosmic winds blow.

The moon rolls a ball made of light,
While crickets compose tunes of delight.
They tickle the air,
With giggles to share,
As the stars join the whimsy-filled night.

Spheres of Serenity

A comet zips by, full of cheer,
Pulling pranks on the stars so near.
With wiggles and swoops,
And tumble of hoops,
It tickles the dark, brings good cheer.

Planets gather for tea in a line,
Discussing the best ways to shine.
Saturn spills tea,
While Pluto agrees,
That it's fun being part of the design.

A quokka waves from the bright moon,
With a smile that could light up a room.
He sings of their day,
In a humorous way,
While the stars join in, flashing bloom.

Galaxies swirl in a dance,
While meteors giggle and prance.
With glittering grace,
They brush past in space,
Creating a waltz-like romance.

Moonlit Laughter

In the glow of the night's silvery sheen,
Bunnies in pajamas bounce and preen.
They tumble and roll,
With all of their soul,
Making merry in moonlit scenes.

A wise old owl tells a joke,
To a fox, who just can't help but choke.
With feathers and fur,
They giggle and purr,
Underneath the soft moonbeam cloak.

Fireflies twinkle like tiny stars,
While waving to friends from afar.
Their laughter rings clear,
Bringing joy and good cheer,
As they dance in their Jupiter cars.

The crescent moon grins like a cat,
As solar winds whisper and chat.
With comets on trails,
And sparkling fails,
The night wraps them up in a mat.

Radiating Radiance

A star tripped and fell in delight,
Landed straight on a comet's flight.
They giggled and spun,
Under rays of the sun,
Creating a glorious sight.

Nebulas swirl like cotton candy,
Dancing wild in the sky, oh so dandy.
They tickle the light,
In colors so bright,
Making evenings sweet and handy.

The moon throws a bash every night,
Inviting all galaxies to sight.
With laughter and fun,
They shine in the sun,
Creating a wonderful light.

Asteroids chase each other round,
While comets make whimsical sound.
In this cosmic spree,
It's plain to see,
That joy in the heavens is found.

Silversmith Silliness

In a shop with pots and pans,
A silversmith danced with fans.
He slipped on a spoon,
And howled at the moon,
Turning gold into silver plans.

With hammers and chisels in tow,
His laughter began to grow.
He fashioned a cat,
Who wore a nice hat,
And wanted to put on a show.

A teapot began to sing,
As he crafted a marvelous thing.
It spun like a top,
Then went for a hop,
While silver and giggles took wing.

The moon watched with joy from above,
For silliness fit like a glove.
In the light of the night,
They danced with delight,
Creating a tableau of love.

Laughter at the Lull

At dusk when the shadows grow long,
The nighttime began with a song.
With owls in the trees,
And whispers of breeze,
The laughter just couldn't be wrong.

A rabbit wore glasses so round,
In a coat that was quite profound.
He juggled bright moons,
And swapped out his spoons,
As giggles and giggles abound.

Beneath the soft glow of the stars,
A squirrel played games with his jars.
He tossed them in glee,
Like a wild jubilee,
In his own little world with no bars.

The crickets struck up a nice tune,
While everyone danced by the moon.
With laughter so bright,
It lasted till light,
As folks joined the night in a swoon.

.

Gleeful Gleams

In a garden where flowers took flight,
The bees buzzed with glee every night.
They wore little hats,
And danced with the cats,
Making mischief till dawn's early light.

A frog on a lily pad sat,
With a pink polka-dot on his hat.
He croaked out a tune,
To the stars up at noon,
And summoned a giggling chat.

With fireflies twirling around,
The raccoons waltzed with a sound.
They slipped and they tripped,
As laughter just zipped,
Till the whole garden shimmered and found.

In each shadow, a chuckle took flight,
As the moon glimmered soft and white.
With glee on display,
They danced till the day,
In a world full of joy and delight.

Echoes of Euphoria

In valleys where echoes would play,
A party went on every day.
With folks in a line,
All dancing in time,
Their laughter could be heard from away.

A pig wore a tutu so bright,
He twirled in the warm, golden light.
With each funky move,
The crowd sought to prove,
That joy gave the best kind of fright.

A goat played a fiddle with flair,
While chickens all clucked in the air.
They formed a great band,
With rhythms so grand,
Creating a joyful affair.

From mountains to shores, joy spread,
As laughter and giggles were fed.
With grins ear to ear,
They banished all fear,
In echoes that danced from the red.

Elysian Laughter

A rabbit danced beneath the glow,
With carrot dreams that stole the show.
He leaped from crater, laughed at the night,
While stars giggled, oh what a sight!

A turtle joined, real slow but proud,
Said, "I'm the king, of this odd crowd!"
The fox in a suit, tried to look grand,
But tripped on moonbeams, oh how he spanned!

The owl gave jokes, a hoot or two,
"Why did the cheese refuse to strew?"
He winked and paused, the punchline soared,
As laughter echoed, a cosmic chord!

So gather round, on this funny sphere,
With creatures bizarre, let out a cheer!
For laughter blooms in the silvery light,
In Elysian realms, all is just right!

Moonstruck Musings

A cat in a hat, quite stylish indeed,
Pondered the moon, in splendidly speed.
"Why don't the stars ever play tag?"
He mused aloud, then started to wag!

An alien child, with eight squid-like legs,
Fell over his thoughts, like toppled eggs.
He chuckled and said, "Let's dance, my friend,
On stardust paths, where giggles blend!"

Shooting stars raced with a comet's flair,
Chasing their tails through the cosmic air.
"Be careful!" cried one, with a wink so bright,
"Too much fun can cause a delightful plight!"

With each odd quirk, under lunar beams,
Life spins like wisps in whimsical dreams.
Embrace your laugh, let it twirl and spin,
With moonstruck joy, let the night begin!

Gleeful Glimmers

A bear wore a tutu, and twirled with glee,
Flat on his back, he said, "Look at me!"
The fireflies buzzed, brought cheers and spark,
Dancing in circles, brightening the dark!

A frog recited poems with flair,
While munching on flies, without a care.
"Ribbit, oh ribbit!" he sang to the tune,
As laughter erupted beneath the moon!

Two squirrels debated, who's fastest of all,
One claimed the title, with a mighty tall wall.
But the other just winked, "I'll race you around,
And if I win, bring me acorns unbound!"

In twinkling laughter, the night came alive,
With each silly act, together they thrive.
So join the fun, let your worries depart,
In gleeful glimmers, we twinkle in heart!

The Midnight Mirths

At midnight, when laughter found its way,
A penguin in slippers began to sway.
He slipped on ice, with a comical cheer,
As friends from afar all gathered near!

A moon cow mooed in a voice so deep,
Singing sweet lullabies, while others would leap.
"Why not join in? Belch out your tune!"
And they did, under the bright, merry moon!

An octopus juggled, with arms all aglow,
Revealing blue fish in a fabulous show.
"Watch out!" yelled a crab, with a pinch and a wink,
As mirthful giggles made the sea creatures blink!

So venture out, where the weird is the norm,
In midnight mirths, where laughter is born.
Let joyful echoes lift your heart's plight,
For life's too short, dance through the night!

Heavenly Hijinks

In the sky where the starlings play,
The moon wears a hat that's too gay.
It tips left and right,
Causing quite a fright,
As it dances the night away!

Shooting stars take a tumble and roll,
While comets race on a stroll.
With winks and with grins,
They dodge all the sins,
Of a night that's beyond any goal!

An owl shared a joke with a bat,
Who hissed with a splash and a spat.
They cackled and cried,
In a world wide and wide,
Where all of the nonsense is sat!

And so up in the cosmic bazaar,
Frogs croon and planets don't spar.
With the joy they emit,
You can't help but sit,
And chuckle beneath a bright star!

Nighttime Nonsense

In the silence of midnight's embrace,
A hedgehog started a race.
With snails as his crew,
They sped past the dew,
Creating a welcoming space!

A cat with a hat made of cheese,
Danced about with the utmost of ease.
He twirled and he spun,
Having way too much fun,
While the mice shouted out, "Oh, please!"

A firefly wore sunglasses so bright,
Claiming, "I'm the star of the night!"
With each little blink,
He made others think,
That he was the best-sparkle light!

Amongst all the laughter and cheer,
Moonbeams pop fizz, they appear!
In the madcap delight,
Of the whimsical night,
All the silliness draws ever near!

Glee of the Nightingale

A nightingale perched on a branch,
Sipped moonlight with a curious glance.
With songs that would soar,
He crooned evermore,
In a whimsical, tuneful romance.

With giggles on every note sung,
Old stars joined in, and they swung.
They twinkled in glee,
As the night danced with tea,
And the cosmos with laughter was stung!

In the shadows a rabbit with flair,
Wore a polka-dot vest and a pair.
He taught all the birds,
To dance their own words,
In a frolicsome, joyous affair!

So heed not the dreary or glum,
For the night plays a magical drum.
As the music takes flight,
And the stars shine so bright,
Join the laughter, and let your heart hum!

Whimsical Wandering

Underneath a canopy of dreams,
A squirrel juggled with moonbeams.
With acorns that twirled,
And the whole world swirled,
In a folly of fancies and schemes.

A firefly buzzed with a tune,
Chasing shadows beneath the moon.
With laughter so bold,
And stories retold,
They danced 'til the break of the noon!

An elf wearing sneakers so bright,
Decided to race through the night.
With laughter and cheer,
He brought all near,
To witness the whimsical sight!

When the dawn peeked with orange and pink,
The creatures paused just to think.
As the day took its claim,
In the night, oh the same,
The joy still continued, a wink!

www.ingramcontent.com/pod-product-compliance
Lightning Source LLC
Chambersburg PA
CBHW071816160426
43209CB00003B/109